The Secret Life of the Red Fox

Laurence Pringle   Illustrated by Kate Garchinsky

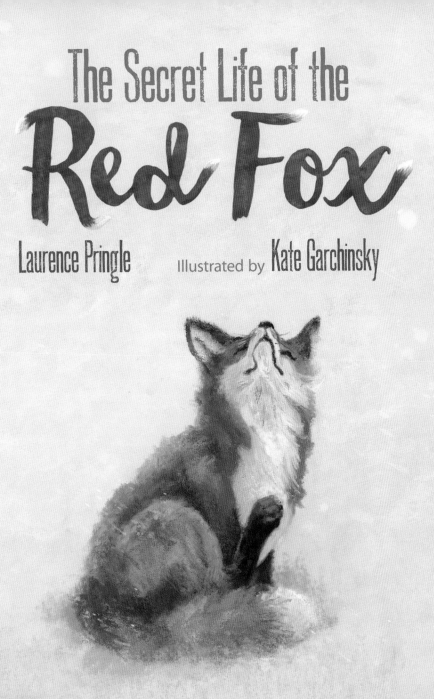

BOYDS MILLS PRESS

AN IMPRINT OF HIGHLIGHTS

Honesdale, Pennsylvania

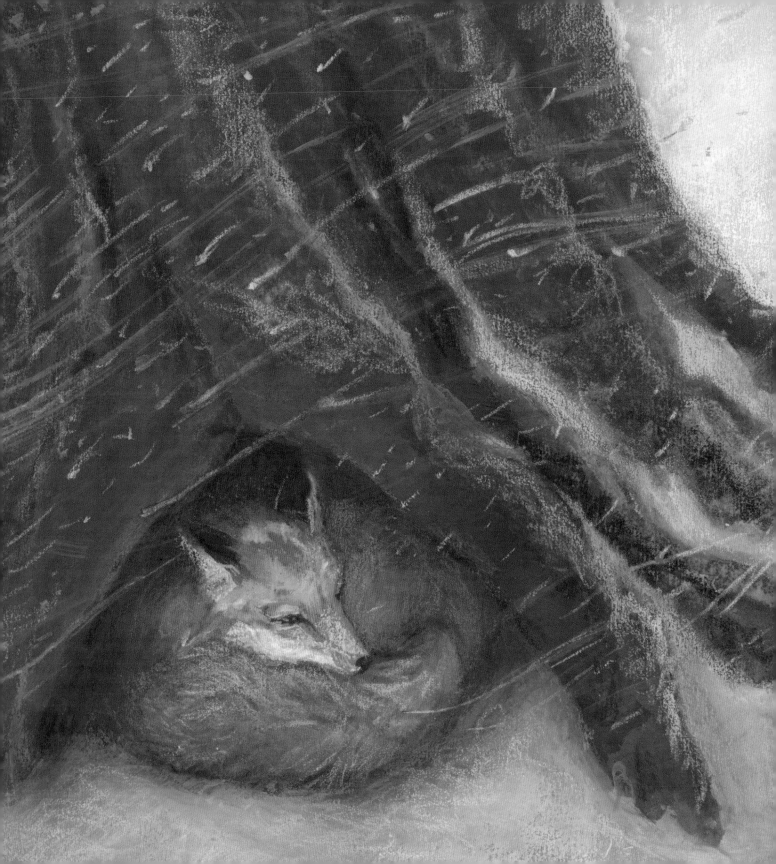

Vixen awakes from a nap.

She is surrounded by snow but feels cozy. She is curled up, and her long, fluffy tail covers her body like a blanket. Her secret hideout faces southwest, inviting sunrays on a February afternoon.

Vixen stands and stretches. She looks and listens all around. She sniffs the air. A fox is a *canine*, related to dogs and wolves. Canines have supersensitive noses and ears. Vixen can smell faint odors and hear tiny sounds that a human would never notice.

Feeling hungry, Vixen sets off on a hunt.

In the snow, her back feet usually land right in the marks made by her front feet, so she leaves a single line of footprints in the snow. Fresh snowflakes dot her russet winter coat, and Vixen's white-tipped tail floats behind her like a banner.

Foxes are *omnivores*, which means they eat both animal and plant food. But in winter Vixen finds no berries or other plant foods to eat. Now she is mostly a *predator*, hunting animals. She explores a thicket where rabbits often hide, but finds no *prey*. She grows more and more hungry.

In a snow-covered meadow, she moves slowly. She pauses and listens, then walks a few steps and stops to listen again. Hidden beneath a foot of snow, a meadow mouse chews on grasses. It makes tiny sounds: *nibble, nibble, nibble.*

Carefully, Vixen steps closer. She moves her head slightly to better pinpoint the sound. *Nibble, nibble, nibble.* She crouches, then leaps high in the air and dives into the snow, leading with her head and front feet. The mouse is caught, and soon eaten. All that remains is a little spot of blood on the snow.

Vixen hunts by day or night, but especially near dawn and dusk. She is cautious, and rarely seen. To most people, her life is a secret.

Today she explores near barns and other farm buildings, where rats and mice may live. Soon Vixen is so well fed that she stores food for another time. She digs a hole in the snow and drops a mouse in. Then she pushes snow with her nose to hide the mouse. She will return to this *cache* of food later.

Nearby, a dog is let outdoors. With its keen canine nose it smells fresh fox scent and barks with excitement. The dog's owner is puzzled. "What are you barking about?"

Near dawn, Vixen hears a special wild bark. It is her mate. She answers, and soon they meet and say hello, as foxes do, by touching and sniffing. They have been a mated pair for several weeks, but often rest and hunt alone. They stay in touch, sending wild foxy calls into the night. And wherever they travel, they leave spots of urine. These scent marks can be messages between Vixen and her mate. To other red foxes the urine marks send a warning: "Stay away. This is our family *territory*!"

Today the foxes trot to an old apple orchard. Apples that fell to the ground last autumn froze in the winter, but now they soften as the days grow warmer. The foxes feast on apples.

One afternoon, Vixen rests alone at the edge of a forest. She scratches at a flea. Her ears perk up at a strange jingling sound. Then she hears other sounds—of animals running hard, breathing hard.

Vixen senses danger. She leaps to her feet, turns, runs. The jingling sound is made by dog collars. Two big dogs are hot on her trail!

She dashes through the woods, crosses a road, leaps onto the top of a stone wall, and looks back. The dogs are still coming. Vixen runs on. She slips through a thicket of thorny brambles.

She leaps across a creek and climbs to the top of a steep hill in a cow pasture. There she catches her breath. Vixen looks out over part of the territory that she knows so well. She sees no dogs. They gave up long ago, outrun and outsmarted.

In the next few days, Vixen visits some abandoned animal burrows. With her front feet she clears dead leaves from the entrance of each one. She crawls underground to investigate. Vixen especially likes one burrow on a sunny hillside with scattered trees. It has two entrances, like a front and back door. Underground, Vixen digs to make the den a little roomier. Then she sets off to go hunting with her mate.

As the spring air warms and the earth turns green, the two foxes often hunt together. One day, Vixen goes into her den and stays, day and night. Sometimes she emerges to stretch her legs and go for a drink. Then she slips underground again. Her mate brings mice, chipmunks, and any other prey he caught. Sometimes he brings *carrion*, like the leg of a dead raccoon he found on a road. He drops the food at the den entrance and makes a quick chortling sound: "Wuk, wuk, wuk, wuk." Vixen comes out to eat.

One spring morning, Vixen leaves for a short hunt. While she's gone, new sounds come from the den: little growls and yips. One by one, four baby foxes cautiously scramble out.

Vixen gave birth to these *kits* about four weeks ago. Newborn, their eyes were closed, and their bodies were covered with short gray hairs. Vixen gave them milk and the warmth of her body. Now they are growing sandy-brown coats of fur. They are bright eyed, bushy tailed, and very curious about the big world above ground.

Both parents work hard to catch enough food for all. Sometimes Vixen stands still, allowing her kits to nurse. The kits nap, wrestle, and sometimes play tug-of-war with a raccoon leg bone. They grow stronger and bolder. They find wild strawberries to eat, and they catch beetles and earthworms—their first prey!

Gradually the kits are *weaned*, no longer fed their mother's milk. Taught by their parents, they learn to find their own food. By midsummer the young foxes have new red coats. They know how to catch mice and grasshoppers in fields. They know where to find wild grapes. And they learn how to be quiet and wary, and lead secret lives.

In early autumn, the young foxes say goodbye to their parents, as foxes do, by touching and sniffing. They leave to seek their own territories. Vixen watches them go, red coats ablaze, their white-tipped tails floating behind them like banners.

More About the Red Fox

The red fox is Earth's most widely distributed wild predatory land mammal. It lives in North and Central America, Europe, Asia, Northern Africa, and Australia.

Red foxes were once less common in North America. Forests covered much of the continent, and red foxes do best in a habitat that is a mix of woods and open land. They were also preyed upon by wolves and coyotes. The situation improved for red foxes when European colonists arrived. The colonists killed many of the large predators and cleared forests for farms. Red foxes began to thrive.

A red fox weighs only about as much as a house cat (8 to 12 pounds, rarely up to 15 pounds). However, the fox's long legs, long-haired fur coat, and long, fluffy tail make it look bigger than a cat. A female fox is called a vixen, and the male is called a dog. Young foxes are called kits, and sometimes pups or cubs.

Most of the time, in all kinds of weather, foxes rest above ground. But very young foxes would be defenseless there, so females use dens during breeding season. Foxes can dig their own burrows in fairly soft soils, but they often take over an existing den dug by a woodchuck or badger.

Vixen's story mentions a few fox sounds. Foxes make a great variety of calls, including whines, woofs, chirps, chortles, and barks. Fox barks have a wild, edgy quality, unlike dog barks. The most unusual call is a high-pitched shriek or scream. Female foxes usually give this call during spring and early summer. The sound warns her kits of danger so they can flee back to their den.

Although foxes are related to wolves and other members of the dog, or canine, family, they are sometimes called "the catlike canine." They are like cats in many ways, including:

- Like cats, foxes have longer whiskers than dogs. As with cats, foxes' whiskers may help them "feel" as they catch and kill prey.

- Both cats and foxes have long, sharp canine teeth they use to pierce and kill small prey animals. Other members of the dog family have thicker, blunt canine teeth, and usually kill small prey animals by shaking them violently.

- Foxes and cats can partly retract, or pull in, their front claws, unlike dogs. Foxes and cats also have small toe pads and hairy feet, which are best for quiet stalking. Most other canines have claws that do not retract, and big toe pads that are best for hard running.

- Like cats, foxes hunt alone. Many other canines hunt in family groups, or packs.

- Like cats, foxes often hunt by slow, close-to-the-ground stalking and also by leaping and pouncing, similar to a cat's hunting style. Other canines often hunt by running down their prey.

- While dogs' eyes have round pupils, both foxes' and cats' eyes have vertical pupils. Foxes also have a layer of shiny tissue in the back of their eyes that helps give them excellent night vision, a trait they also share with cats.

Foxes are known for their intelligence and cunning. If you outsmart someone, you "outfox" them. A sly red fox is often a character in fiction. Foxes have inspired many trickster stories in cultures all over the world.

Long ago, foxes sometimes killed free-ranging chickens, but today most poultry is confined and protected. But red foxes can do great harm when they are brought to places where they do not naturally live. In Australia, nonnative red foxes harm populations of small mammals and ground-nesting birds. In California, red foxes from the Midwestern United States were released into lowlands and shore areas, where they had never lived before. Like in Australia, these nonnative foxes are a threat to populations of ground-nesting birds. In both California and Australia, steps are now being taken to reduce numbers of red foxes in order to protect the native animals.

Still, throughout most of the red fox's vast range on Earth, this little wild dog is welcomed and admired for its beauty, grace, and intelligence.

Glossary

Cache: a hiding place for something valuable. The word can also describe an action, for example, "The fox stopped to cache a dead mouse."

Canine, *or* canid: a member of the animal family *Canidae*, which includes dogs, wolves, coyotes, jackals, and foxes. The long, pointy teeth in the upper and lower jaws of many mammals—including humans—are also called canines.

Carrion: an already dead animal that is eaten by other animals

Kit: a young fox, sometimes called a pup or cub. The young of some other mammals, including beavers, are also called kits.

Omnivore: an animal that eats both plants and animals

Predator: an animal that hunts and eats other animals

Prey: an animal that is hunted by other animals for food

Territory: the area in which an animal lives and defends against others of the same species. Many wild mammals and birds have territories, especially in the times they raise young.

Vixen: a female fox

More Books About Foxes

Green, Jen. *Red Fox*. Danbury, CT: Grolier, 2008.

Henry, J. David. *Red Fox: The Catlike Canine*. Washington, D.C.: Smithsonian, 1996.

Henry, J. David. *How To Spot a Fox*. Shelburne, VT: Chapters, 1993.

Nobleman, Marc Tyler. *Foxes*. Tarrytown, NY: Benchmark, 2007.

Read, Tracy. *Exploring the World of Foxes*. Buffalo, NY: Firefly, 2010.

Wallace, Karen. *Red Fox*. Cambridge, MA: Candlewick, 1994.

Dedicated to my first grandchild, welcoming her to our family and wishing her a life full of adventure, discovery, and love. —LP

For Mom, Dad, and all the younger kits in my hidden fox family: Maureen, Claire, Andy, Meggie, and Ryan. —KG

Special thanks to Kent Brown for drawing the ley lines between the author and illustrator.

The author thanks J. David Henry, PhD, author of *Red Fox: The Catlike Canine*, *How to Spot a Fox*, and *Foxes: Living on the Edge*, for his careful review of the text and illustrations.

Text copyright © 2017 by Laurence Pringle
Illustrations copyright © 2017 by Kate Garchinsky
All rights reserved.
For information about permission to reproduce selections from this book, contact permissions@highlights.com.

BOYDS MILLS PRESS
An Imprint of Highlights
815 Church Street
Honesdale, Pennsylvania 18431
boydsmillspress.com
Printed in China

ISBN: 978-1-62979-260-6
Library of Congress Control Number: 2016942352
First edition
Production by Sue Cole
10 9 8 7 6 5 4 3 2 1

The text of this book is set in Mercurious CT Light.
The illustrations are done in pastels and aqua crayons on sanded paper.